Charles C. Van Zandt

Newport Ballads

Charles C. Van Zandt

Newport Ballads

ISBN/EAN: 9783744789073

Printed in Europe, USA, Canada, Australia, Japan

Cover: Foto ©Thomas Meinert / pixelio.de

More available books at **www.hansebooks.com**

Newport Ballads

BY

CHARLES C. VAN ZANDT.

PUBLISHED BY THE
Newport Historical Society.
1894.

Polly Tilley's Shop.

Do you remember, Tom, my boy !
  Near forty years ago,
A frosty, star-gemmed Christmas Eve—
  The ground all white with snow ?
Like shooting stars down Pelham street
  We coasted on a sled—
You wore a dogs-eared, coon-skin cap ;
  And mine was worsted, red.
You jammed your old blue mitten down
  Your pocket, and with glee
Showed me your tender mother's gift.
  A four pence ha' penny.
I had three coppers old and brown,
  And so with slide and hop,
We went through Spring street on the run
  To Polly Tilley's shop!

I see it now, the little shop,—
  So queer and old and quaint,
The iron latch, where eager hands
  Had rubbed off all the paint,
The door, with glass in upper half,

That jarred and rang a bell;
The little counter with a rail,
That we remember well;
It was as bright as holly leaves,
And on its dainty top,
The golden candy rested sweet,
In Polly Tilley's shop.

There peppermint and sassafras
And fragrant wintergreen,
And lemon, with a tawny stripe,
Deliciously were seen;—
In shallow pans of unctuous tin,
Worked with the tenderest care,
Molasses candy's flaxen links,
Gleamed like Godiva's hair.
Oh! Tom, this dizzy chase for fame
And gold, we'd better drop:—
While memory points, with lingering love
To Polly Tilley's shop!

The little shelves were filled with bowls
Of herbs, and all the ills
That Godfrey's Cordial left, were cured
By Dean's Rheumatic Pills;

Some huckleberries bathed in gin,
   And other doctor's stuff,—
With two fat quaker-colored jars
   Of Scotch and yellow snuff,
A modest case of brass-knobbed drawers,
   All decked in living green,
Were labelled nutmegs, cloves and spice,
   Too precious to be seen—
And when the bell began the ring,
   Out Betsey Stanley 'd pop,
With clean checked apron, to attend
   On Polly Tilley's shop !

Alack a day ! that times should change,
   As years go coasting down,
For Christmas Eve comes just the same
   To Newport's olden town,—
The sweet bells ring, the children sing,
   The windows smile with light,
And Bethlehem's diamond star is there,
   Upon the breast of night.
A boy comes dashing down the hill,
   Upon his painted sled,
But you and I are at the foot,
   And Polly Tilley's dead.

Perhaps, a skillful hand might glean
From memory's golden sheaves.
Some fairer pictures to adorn
The pleasant winter eves :
But there is nothing left on earth,
To ring on Christmas chimes,
Like the clear, crystal, silvery notes,
Of childhood's blessed times.
But Fame's long hill is very steep :
We stagger toward the top,
And every step but leaves behind
Good Polly Tilley's shop !

The Little Old Woman.

There's a little old woman lives over the way,
In a gambrel-roofed cottage unpainted and grey,
And where the brown grape vine is climbing across,
The shingles are covered with patches of moss.

By the wood fire-side in the winter she sits,
In a list bottomed rocker, and sings as she knits,
In a quavering voice with a tremulous croon,
And the click of her needle keeps time to the tune.

Her Bible she reads, slowly turning the leaves,
And she garners bright grain from its beautiful
    sheaves;
And the tears dim her eyes, as she lifts them on
    high,
In search of her treasure laid up in the sky.

In her best Sunday gown, whether ailing, or well,
She trots to her meeting at sound of the bell,
And she sits in her pew, like a wren on a perch,
This little grey dame in a Puritan church.

Our very old people remember, they think,
When her hair was as glossy and black as a mink,
And her cheeks red as roses, her teeth white as
    pearls,
And this little old woman the fairest of girls.

She had a dear lover, alack and a day!
A sailor, who sailed from the beautiful bay ;
And the summers may blush and the winters may
    pale,
But their sun never shines on his home-coming sail.

At a little round table from over the sea,
She sits at the sunset and pours out her tea,
And the delicate cup and its saucer are white
As a floating pond lily, just kissed by the light.

And a ship under sail, with its flag at the mast,
All laden with memories brought from the past,
Is painted upon them, as life like and fair,
As the mirage that floats in the orient air.

His ship that he sailed in, his sweetheart to wed,
By others forgotten—the sunset grows red—
But the little old woman just murmurs a prayer,
And smiles as she knows that her lover is there.

But a day will soon come when the lilac's perfume,
Through the half open window will float through
the room,
And the house will be quiet, and she be at rest,
With a single white rose on her motionless breast.

And the angels will come with their glittering
wings,
While the parson he prays, and the choir it sings,
And bear to the home that is fairer than day,
The little old woman from over the way.

Carrier's New Year's Address.

NEWPORT DAILY NEWS, JANUARY, 1867.

Old Newport! queenly City by the Sea!
Home of our childhood, and our golden prime!
Enchanted Island, where ripe, silvery age
Melts into heaven, its full accomplished time
All crowned with glory, its three score and ten
Graced with another score of whiter years
Gathered from heaven itself—so our old men
Round their long lives with sleep, and we shed tears.
Beautiful City! in the New Year's time,
Fragrant with memories of the Old Year fled,
Standing like Moses in his priestly robes
Between the living and the sainted dead,
As the last hours grow shivering, cold, and small,
Like dwarfs that bear the dead Year to its grave;
I hear the ancient State House clock strike *Twelve*,
And Trinity's white spire that trembling gave
It's ringing vesper notes at nine o'clock,
Strikes out upon its brazen bell the Year.
And in its shadow sleep the silent dead—
Where   crumbling   monuments   their   moss-grown
    tablets rear,

Wrap the dead year in snow, 'tis not more cold
Than his white icy face ; the glittering frost
Will melt in tears when morning dawns, because
His old, old friend of many days is lost.

       *   *   *   *

    Hurrah! Hurrah! from the afar
    The New Year trips along!
    A rosy boy, with shouts of joy,
    And peals of jocund song.
    His eyes are bright as stars at night,
    His lips are cherry red,
    His dancing feet in twinkles meet ;
    He tosses back his head—
    All crowned with holly's glossy leaves,
    And scarlet berries fair.
    He shouts a glorious chorus forth
    Upon the frosty air,
    And the drowsy, tired Carrier
    Of the "*Newport Daily News*"
    Woke up and heard the curious sound,
    And then put on his shoes,
    Buttoned his ancient sack well up,
    Mounted his threadbare cap—
    For he and they just roused from sleep,
    Had lost their early nap—

And sallied out to find the watch,
All in their snug retreats,
To stop this roystering youngster
Who was "revelling in the streets"
And have him up next morning,
For his very ill-timed sport,
To be well fined and then "sent up"
Before the Justice's Court.
But he had only jogged along
A square or two, or so,
When New Year leaped upon his back,
And struck him quite a blow,
And gave a shout, and rubbed his ears,
And punched him in the side,
And laughed until the old streets rang,
And then aloud he cried—
"What! Ho! my lovely carrier dove,
Whither so early bound?
The morning reddens in the sky,
And strews its roses radiantly
Upon the snow clad ground.
The old Year's dead, it can't be helped;
He did some things quite well:
He left you poor! how sad that is—
You best of all can tell.

If I was you, I'd get myself
Out of these little messes,
By making, though its rather cold—
A few New Year's air-dresses!
Then take them 'round, when folks feel well,
Just after a good dinner,
And they'll *shell out* like human be-ans—
And you'll alone be winner—
I'll go ahead with magic key;
Where there's a puckering pocket,
With Greenbacks verdant in its depths,
I'll cautiously unlock it "—
And then he vanished—here I am
Poor as Job's leanest turkey—
Which was a goose; or he'd been rich.
I've been obliged to work a
Great many hours turning wheels;
One good turn needs another:
I've walked long miles, in heat and cold :
I've had a sight of bother
To find out where on earth you lived,
So I could leave the paper,
And some folks move so frequently,
It seems a natural caper.
Here are my rhymes; the rime of age

Is glistening on my hair ;
If you're *averse* to verse like this,
I think it only fair—
To give a little fluttering script.
With generous hand and will.
When I, a sort of carrier dove,
Peck with my annual bill,
And wish you all in hearts and homes,
Peace, happiness, and cheer,
God's blessing which is all in all--
To bring a glad New Year.

The Old Fountain.

Farewell! ancient Fountain of granite so gray,
Under yonder great Elm, where we all loved to
  play,
Where the bright water bubbled its melodies sweet,
Overflowing its bowl to the cattle's brown feet.
Here the dust-worn, and thirsty, bent over and drank
From the chained iron ladle which seemed to say
  ' Thank,'
As all dripping it fell with a musical clank,
And the bare-footed boys so caressingly rub
Their little brown hands on the moss covered tub.
Here " Jowler " all panting with summer's red heat,
Laps up the cool stream as it bathes his fore feet,
While his hind ones extended are cooling below,
Where baptised by its spray, the green water weeds
  grow.
Here old Thurston Almy, at daybreak would come,
And draw a clean pail for his old Medford Rum,
And tall Dr. Case would stride over the curbs
And bear off a gallon to mix with his herbs.
Our friend Gov. Lawton, could come as he'd please,
To water the Mall with its just planted trees.

And good Charlie Feke who was humpbacked and
   queer,
But always to Charity lent a kind ear,
Would lead some poor child he had fed to the
   place,
And with motherly hand wash the tears from his
   face ;
And the Angel looked down who is brighter than
   Fame,
On the cup of cold water in Jesus' dear name.
Old Corey's white truck horse that scarcely can
   stand,
With the check rein unloosed by his trembling
   hand,
Dips his nose in the Fountain and dreams of good
   grain,
Switches off a big fly and is youthful again.
As straight as an arrow, with quick sinewy stride,
Doctor Hazard comes over, to plunge in the tide
His great cedar pail, to refresh the forlorn,
Swollen faced, weeping urchin, whose tooth he has
   drawn,
How kindly he looks as the bright waters shine,
And he hums to himself bending down, "Auld
   Lang Syne."

At eleven o'clock, from the brass knockered door,
Which Commodore Perry has opened before,
Comes Governor Collins with bottle and cup,
And good Parson Eddy is following him up,
Who says as they drink to the clock's silvery chime,
Why! *if ever I drink* 'tis about this ere time!"
Here's a flock of blue pigeons with murmuring coo,
And their little red feet are all spangled with dew ;
They alight, and they drink, turn their heads to the
  sky
As if to give thanks, then away they all fly.
Here comes a calm Quaker, 'tis old Stephen Gould,
For his sponge must be wet and his irons be cooled ;
He has a blue coat, faced with buff, done to-night,
For Nathanael Green, who is going to fight.
Farewell! ancient Fountain, old Newport stands by
With bandanna in hand, and a mist in his eye,
And drops his salt tears in the water that flows,
Drop by drop, from the new fountain's cast iron nose.
And the woman that stands like a brazen faced lass,
And tries to make iron look something like brass,
Would weep if she could, down the green paint
  she dons,
In wretched attempts to seem something like
  bronze :

And how it must heighten the depths of her woe
That she never can even be " *in statue quo*,"
Cast irony only on art and on sense,
A humbug, a folly, a sham, a pretense.
The pigeons are dying with heat and with thirst,
And the water is dammed when the Fountain is
  cursed,
Each dog with his tongue hanging out of his
  mouth,
Licks the rust off the base and is panting with
  drought,
For the basin is shallow and clear out of reach,
Like the waters of Life that the High Churchmen
  preach.
Ye good City Fathers, now list to my prayer
Take the cast iron woman and run her for Mayor,
She was run in the mould, and her powers don't
  wane,
I see no good reason, she can't run again.

Prologue.

TO THE DEDICATION OF THE OPERA HOUSE IN
PROVIDENCE.

———

Bright fairy Puck! swifter than rifle shot,
   Put round the earth, thy girdle spun of light,
And tie it in a jewelled lover's knot ;
   There by the footlights—on the stage to-night.
'Tis done—it swings as musical as chimes
   Of "sweet bells," never "jangling out of tune,"
A star-beam ladder—how the fairy climbs
   To dress his elf locks in the mirror moon.
Now Puck! leap down ; don't bump your little head
   On the proscenium, you may break a bone—
Or singe your silver wings, or worse, instead
   B flat by falling in the big trombone ;
Here, take my hand, stretch up on your tip-toe
   Stop winking at the girls— the men will hiss!
You've lived forever! now I want to know
   What Roger Williams would have thought of this?
Why when he landed on the Seekonk shore,
   The Indians said " *What Cheer?*" and its but fair
To think if he was with us now once more,
   He'd say " I'll take the best orchestra *chair!* "

For, after his long life, so Orthodox—
  His very bones don't fill a *private box* "
Yet I believe that stalwart Baptist bore ;
  Wit brightening wisdom 'neath his thatch of gray,
And would have loved the stage, and cried encore !
Although he travelled in another way,
Never by *stage*—but made *tracts* on the shore—
  Come Puck ! trot out your memories from their
    cloisters,
These *opening* nights are death to rhymes and
    oysters.

      *   *   *   *   *

    Throwing up his dimpled heels,
    Turning somersaults and wheels,
    Every feather in his wings
    Like a song-bird trills and sings ;
    Dancing eyes, like diamonds bright,
    Tangled curls of sunrise light,
    Teeth as white as snow drops are,
    Laugh like music from a star,
    Cheeks as red as sunset hue,
    Breath like violets wet with dew,
    Little Puck paints fair and fast,
    Mystic pictures from the past.

      *   *   *   *

My Lords and Ladies, for upon my word,
Each Yankee is a lady or a lord ;
The night was dark, a gale was rising fast,
And Newport's spires quivered in the blast,
When in a little building by the shore,
Half deafened by the Equinoctial roar,
A band of players from across the sea,
Acted a queer, old-fashioned comedy—
Giving their earnings to sweet charity.
There first upon our fields the buskin trod,
Where beaded moccasins had pressed the sod ;
And there, a century since the fair Muse bore
Her first glad offspring on New England's shore.
Your city has a pleasant pictured page,
In history for her annals of the stage,
Radiant with stars, how brilliant seems forsooth,
The kingly splendor of the elder Booth ;
Whether with tragedy he rent the air,
Or with a tender pathos, rich and rare,
Gave a new music to the Lord's own prayer.
Old men are living now, who loved to meet
George Frederick Cook upon the busy street ;
Heard Hackett roar in Falstaff, or perchance,
Finn flash his wit's electric pointed lance ;

Seen Charles Kean's Hamlet, and young Forest's
  Lear,
And mad Joe Cowell, play his pranks so queer;
Heard Conway's voice, who sleeps beneath the wave,
Or Hazard's fire, quenched in an early grave :
Or Charlotte Cushman, seem the blood to freeze
In gaunt, prophetic, weird Meg Merrilles :
Here Taglioni whirled in fire-fly maze,
Madame Augusta flashed between the plays,
Or Fanny Ellsler's sweet, bewitching glance,
Made hearts beat cadence to her airy dance :
And later still, came Howard, Forbes and Drew,
The Palmer's grassy mound is wet with dew.
Old Pardey's nights were crowned with an encore,
And Varrey " set the tables on a roar."
Grace strode the stage superbly, rich in health,
Now he lies palsied—aid him from your wealth !
Three times the Fire fiend flung his blazing torch
Against the lintels of the Theapian porch :
Three times the Drama sank in dark eclipse,
The rosy fruit was ashes on the lips.
A truce to memories ! we have come to-night
With bursts of music and a flood of light,
To dedicate to th' Histronic Muse
This splendid Temple ; not alone we choose

To garland her white limbs and crown her head,
With flowers plucked from the past, but we instead
Would nightly on this mimic stage rehearse,
Great thoughts embalmed in purest prose and verse ;
And elevate the drama from a trade—
To what it was when Shakespeare wrote and played :
Call a glad smile to lips grown white with care :
Show virtue radiant as she is fair ;
Act comedies culled from " the golden age ;"
Retouch with living hues each master's page :
Call Garrick's spirit from across the sea ;
And Siddons, stately Queen of Tragedy.
Then Science, Art, the Drama linked will stand
The Sister Graces of this Western Land.

Fragment from a Poem

READ BEFORE ST. JOHN'S LODGE.

———

What pleasant memories of the past,
  Our ancient masons bring;
What songs of glorious " Auld Lang Syne,"
  Their veteran voices sing.
When first in Newport's sea-girt town,
  Late in the purple fall,
More than a hundred years ago,
  Numbering but twelve in all,
They met within a little room,
  And ere the night was gone,
Had worked a good masonic lodge,
  And named it for St. John.
Many the memories we might call
  To-night, if we stood in their ancient hall :
Many the fête and the whirling dance—
  Many the flashing, thrilling glance—
Many the notes of music sweet,
  Kept to the time of fairy feet—
Many the lovers and ladies all,
  Have danced in the jig in the masons' hall.

John Joe.

"John Joe" was black as an ebony log,
　And straight as a tropical tree,
His teeth were white as the elephant's tusks,
　And his eyes as dark as could be :
Found in a boat, drifting afloat,
　Many long years ago :
Now he is dead, place on his head
　Stone, the two words, "John Joe."

Full well I know he was out of his head,
　And he lived in the poor house, too :
But he was a King in his younger days,
　In the land where the cocoanuts grew.
A mighty Prince and ever since
　Mad fever laid him low,
He's borne a name unknown to fame,
　And simply this : "John Joe."

Yet he had a proud and martial tread,
　When he followed the rattling drum
And the old Artillery's blue platoons ;
　When colored eggs and tin horn tunes,
And ice cream stalls with pewter spoons,

Showed 'Lection Day had come ;
He marched along as straight and strong,
As soldiers in a row,
With sash and plume, but now the tomb,
Holds all left of " John Joe."

On Sunday he went to the meeting house,
Where he listened and prayed and read,
With Bible always upside down,
And never a dream in his head,
Of the Saxon God, or the English words,
Which the preacher mildly said ;
But when they sang, his strong voice rang
In psalms of joy, or woe,
To praise *his* God ; but now the sod
Is over poor " John Joe."

We shall miss him on every gala day ;
With his suit of the stripes and stars,
The tarnished droop of his epaulette,
And his well ground sword with no slaughter wet,
And his chevron's tinselled bars ;
His training's done, trumpet nor gun,
Will wake him, here below ;
But up on high, God's loving eye,
Pities and keeps " John Joe."

Fragment from a Poem

READ BEFORE THE SOCIETY OF THE ARMY OF THE
POTOMAC.

———

Wild rang the singing, for the night was still,
And when it ceased a plaintive whippoorwill
Wailed his sad cry to crickets piping shrill.
Sweet sleep! of all God's blessings the most blest,
Soothes every tired soldier to his rest.

    *   *   *   *   *   *

Bury the past! let memory's snowy wing
Brush all the darkness from the days we sing—
With tender hand when Spring her emerald strews,
Place fragrant flowers, wet with heaven's dews,
Upon the little mound whose broken sod
Shows one bright patriot's spirit gone to God.
Dear is remembrance ; sweet to close my lay
With blossoms culled for Decoration Day.

    With tolling bells, and booming guns,
        And muffled drum-beat's throb :
    With heavy step and shrouded flags,
        Each half-drawn breath a sob ;
    The solemn Army marches through
        The quiet, listening town :

To deck with memory's flowery stars
    The green turned up with brown—

The little mounds of dew-wet grass,
    The chiselled blocks of stone—
Where soldiers rest ; where heroes sleep ;
    Wrapped in the flag—alone !

Ho ! comrade with the single arm,
    Give me a wreath of green
To hang upon this snowy slab ;
    The rain-drop's silvery sheen

Upon its glossy laurel leaves
    Are tears our Mother weeps—
Now some Immortelles for a crown,
    For here our General sleeps.

This is a very little mound,
    He was so young to die—
Give me some rose-buds, and those sprigs
    Of fragrant Rosemary.

Now, brother with the shattered leg,
    Hand me those Hyacinths blue,
To place upon this grassy hill,
    For he was always true.

White, sunrise-flushed Arbutus buds
  Are just the very thing
To sweetly serve the drummer-boy—
  He sleeps in life's young spring.

That Passion-flower of glorious bloom,
  Like him who died to save ;
With these white Lilies, stainless, sweet,
  Rest on the Chaplain's grave.

Those bright Verbenas, perfect red,
  Those Valley Lilies white ;
Those Blue-bells and Forget-me-nots,
  These Daisies starred with light,

Have gathered from the rainbow tints
  Old Glory's stripes and gold—
Her Color Sergeant's grave shall bear
  These fruits of wounds untold.

Some Lavender,--his memory
  Is fragrant,—and a spray
Of that green Cassia let us place
  Upon his tomb today.
He was a Christian, and he loved
  To teach his men to pray.

This man was old, full three-score years,
    When he went forth to fight :
Bring me some Ivy's glossy leaves,
    And full-blown Roses white.

Some scarlet Holly berries here.
    And Mistletoe's green spray ;
This soldier fell in the wild fight
    We had on Christmas day.

A branch of that sweet Orange bloom
    And one red flower—the tide
Of his young life poured out and left
    A broken-hearted bride.

Scatter the flowers we bear around
    The white tents of the dead ;
The night comes down, the day is done.
    The old Flag overhead

Hangs silently and wearily :
    The rain falls on the sod ;
Our loved ones sleep ; how well they died
    For Freedom and for God !

Fragment from Poem

Then the summer is gone, and the harvest is ended,
  The reapers have gathered the glittering grain :
On upland and lowland the snow has descended,
  To crown the glad earth for the Winter King's reign ;
The days growing short at the close of November,
  The nights getting longer, and stronger, and cold,
And at sunset, the windows, like bright glowing embers,
  Are gleaming with rubies, and diamonds, and gold ;
At the dead of the night, when the wind, shrilly
    whistling,
  Is piping a song for the snow and the sleet,
The frost, clad in silver, all sparkling and glistening,
  Creeps through the still city, with snow-muffled feet ;
When the hosts of the stars in their steely-like armor,
  Seem shivering sentinels set in the sky,
Half nodding, then starting to hear the alarmer,
  Then sinking to sleep with a quivering eye.
Far up in the north the red watch-fires burning,
  Now shoot towards the zenith, now flicker away,
Till the warrior, Mars, to his cloud-tent returning,
  Shall change the last watchword of night to the day.

A Cup of Capital T.*

Our ancient dames with spectacles on nose,
Their long checked aprons and old-fashioned clothes
With petticoat and short gown, quaint to see,
Oft read their fortunes in a cup of Tea.
First quaffed the fragrant nectar from the cup,
Then turned the fragile china bottom up,
To read of fortune's kind or stern decree ;--
Simple domestic cup and saucery.
The pleasant art ought never to be lost,
For T's are capital unless they're crost.
Tall men, the high sons of this favored land,
The real he beaux,—Bohea-mian like they stand,
And each dear Amazon with beauty shines
At the command of " Wheeler into lines !"
Tea was the staple when our land was blest,
Cotton now occupies each empty chest,
Tea-dious,--Good heavens ! that can never be,
Tea-deums will reward sweet charity,

*A Cup of Tea drawn from 1773, was served at the Opera
House, August 27, 1875, for the benefit of the sufferers by the
floods in France. It was a *play*, and Mrs. Dr. Wheeler one
most interested in its performance.

And the poor French, like Noah's diluvial host,
When in the flood the rest gave up the ghost,
Will sup with us in real fraternal love
On olive branches, tea, and hot broiled dove.
A cup of tea,—what subject could be finer,
Embalmed in English or in broken china?
And when together we have quaintly supped
No one's been bled though each one has been
   cupped.
A kind of kettle drum, where people meet,
So called because its very hard to beat.
Don't stay away on any foolish ground,
We need some spoons to stir our sweetness round,
And though for charity we fondly yearn
Yet what we make we all expect to urn.
Ring up the curtain, see the old brocade,
That near an hundred years ago was laid
With fragrant odors in its rich folds prest
In the embraces of a camphor chest,
Bright with the glories of a silvery age,
Float, filled with youth, across the lighted stage.
The minuet's cold stately steps they show
As trod by Washington and Rochambeau.
The dazzling lights on curious costumes fall,
That graced cotillions in old Penrose Hall.

And seventy-six with blushing eighteen halts
In the new revolution of a waltz,
When free from war's dread terrors and alarms
We like our fathers still resort to arms.
Row sham beaux on our placid harbors wave,
While brave Rochambeau sleeps within his grave.
And as you speed your shells from shore to shore,
Your love and life like his will all be oar.
And when this play is over and the band,
Crawl underneath the stage with pipes in hand,
Then if we pause before our parting bow,
And ask you how you like it ? answer Howe.

Quaker Meeting.

In our pleasant old town in the sweet month of
   June,
When the trees are in leaf, and the birds are in
   tune,
When the fog its silvery lace work of gossamer
   flings
All broidered with pearls from its phantom-like
   wings;

When it drapes the brown wharves in a mantle of
   mist,
Till the silvery Bay by the sunset is kissed ;
When the great curtain rises in splendor untold,
Like rubies dissolved in a goblet of gold ;

Then in the quaint city, they quietly meet,
These birds of grey plumage, all songless, but
   sweet,
And the dear placid faces so kindly and fair,
Breathe their plain yeas and nays on the sea-fra-
   grant air.

And the rosy checked damsels, bright eyed and
  demure,
Like lilies unfolding, so spring like and pure,
Ripple out a clear laugh from their red lips em-
  pearled,
And dream of the sad luscious sins of the world.

Old men with their broad brims so mouselike and
  sleek,
On the straight backed high seat will religiously
  speak,
And the truths of the Scriptures sedately will
  quote,
In language as smooth as the nap of their coat.

How tender and true are the clear words that fall,
Which the dear Spirit moves them to utter to all ;
How solemn the cadences wave-like and calm,
Like the rythm that rolls through an Israelites
  pslam.

The meeting house ample, unpainted, and bare ,
Seems filled with the glory that silvers the hair,
And floods the still streets, and encircles the lands,
The light of the City not builded with hands.

Charles T. Brooks.

—

We will lay him in the tomb,
When the land is all abloom,
With the roses and the lilies of a golden day in
    June.

And the silver throated chimes,
Up above are chanting rhymes,
And the little birds are singing all in tune.

On so bright a summer day,
How he loved to preach, and pray,
And his words were full of fragrance as the
    flowers;

Now with childhood's tender grace
On his dear unconscious face,
In the old familiar place,
He is sleeping all these quiet summer hours.

With the freshness of a boy,
Flushed with every simple joy,
Unfolding like a daisy in the sun ;

For his life was pure and white,
And his heart was full of light,
And the flower was a star just begun ;

But it faded slow away,
Growing fairer every day,
Till its snowy petals dropt on the sod ;

But the glowing golden heart,
Was transfigured and is part
Of the lights around the throne of our God.

For he certes was a man,
On the bright celestial plan,
Springing out from the strong New England root.

Grace and nature here combine,
As the green leaves and the vine
Bear the amethystine clusters of the fruit.

When Christmas Eve came round,
And the frost was on the ground,
And the winter winds their moans seemed to hush,

How his carols would ring,
And themselves seem to sing
Like a snow bird with the trill of a thrush.

How the poor Carrier Boy,
Has seemed radiant with joy,
As at New Year he journey'd along;

For the heart now so still,
At its own loving will,
Has filled both his hands full of song.

Oh! gentle summer light,
Kiss the lips so cold and white,
And stir the silvered glory of his hair;

No words of grief we speak,
For the roses on his cheek
Are blooming in a land more fair.

" Blessed are the pure in heart!"
How our winged memories start,
And like angels float adown on the breeze;

For his age was perfect youth,
And his life unclouded Truth,
And "although he was blind now he sees."

Fragment from a Masonic Address.

A score of years are passed, and five beside
Have cast their buds and blossoms on the tide
Of Time's swift-flowing and resistless stream,
Like shadowy Angels in a passing dream,
Since a bright morning at the close of June
With roses all in bloom, and birds in tune,
And purple lilacs on the bending trees
Beckoning with perfumed breath the golden bees;
I stood within a pulpit, in a church,
A verdant parrot, on a solemn perch,
And with uncertain voice and visage wan,
Recited verses on the good St. John,
And tried to picture in untutored way
The lodge that bore his name an hundred years
   that day.
I look around, and here and there a face
Set in a frame of silver, bears a trace
Of some vague flitting memory of the day,
I tried to read my first Masonic lay.
The orator who for an hour or more,
Drew richest treasures from his precious store,
And linked them all together clear and bright,

A chain of jewels, glittering with light,
With heart brim full of warm Masonic love,
Has joined his brothers in the Lodge above.
The pleasant bard who wrote the tuneful ode,
And his Pegasus gracefully bestrode,
When all the people rose and sang in time,
Loud, rich, and ringing, as a Christmas chime.
With clouded mind, impatient if it waits,
Plied with his hand the scissors of the Fates,
And left some flowers and bright-hued autumn
    leaves,
But like all poets had few golden sheaves.
Ballou's great lustrous eyes, sincere and true,
That gazed upon me from a neighboring pew,
Closed by the touch of battle's blood-stained hand,
Opened in glory on the better land.
Where are the girls who formed a bright bouquet,
Of pinks and lilies on that pleasant day?
A shade more quiet, but with fragrance yet,
Like Spring's first snow-drops changed to mig-
    nonette.
Mayhap one-half that thronging audience stands,
In the great Lodge above, not made with hands,
With deeper love, and strong emotion stirred,
They hear from His own lips the Master's word,

And pitying look on us who lingering wait,
Poor fellow-craftsmen at the Temple gate.
But I am blundering, like all oldish men,
This is the daughter,—'twas the mother then—
To whom we brought our offerings on that day
When buds and flowers and girls and boys were
    gay,
And Time's illuminated scroll unrolled ,
Showed she was beautous, though a century old.
Men are like watches, very curious cre'tures,
Ought to be *le(a)vers*, but they are *repeaters*,
The few of us who linger yet alive,
Now worship at the shrine of *twenty-five* ;
And sing to-night with just as conscious truth
The love of goodness linked with blushing youth ;
Her cheeks are roses, and her teeth are pearls
And sunshine tangles in her golden curls,
And on her brow a lover's eye can see
Jewels of hope, not stars of memory.
God bless her, when the century counts its gems
And weaves their beauties into diadems,
Sunrise will turn to sunset's radiant red,
And shed its glory on her whitened head.

Onward.

They are marching! onward marching!
  At the Great Commander's call;
We have gathered in the fruitage,
  And the leaves begin to fall.
Some, like blossoms in the Springtime,
  Floated softly to the ground;
But the Autumn leaves are drifting
  With a sad funereal sound.

And the long and glittering column,
  With its vanguard crowned with light,
And its banners bathed in glory,
  They are marching out of sight.
Maimed and crippled, worn and weary,
  Stained with blood, and soiled with rust,
Glossy laurels, civic garlands,
  They are whithering, "dust to dust."

Forward! double quick, the order,
  Father Abraham leads the hosts;
Like the sunset clouds in splendor
  Comes the army of the ghosts.

All the men that fell in battle,
　　All the heroes of the fight,
Praying women, noble statesmen,
　　They are marching out of sight.

And my children ! little children !
　　With your faces bright with youth,
As you watch the thinning army
　　Of the men who fought for truth ;
As you see them fast receding,
　　In the " strange old-fashioned way,"
To the old, whose hair is silvered,
　　It will seem but yesterday,

Since the Southerns rose in madness,
　　And the land was dark with slaves,
And the prairies, and the mountains,
　　And the valleys, yawned with graves;
When our blessed stars were falling,
　　And our eyes were dim with tears,
And winged Time brought every day,
　　A burden filled with years.

Oh ! how beautiful their faces
　　As they left the fireside,
And went drifting from our kisses

At the turning of the tide ;
How the bugles silver snarling
  Drowned the women's last goodbye,
And the drumbeat hushed their foot-falls,
  As they marched away to die !

And the statesmen ! stalwart statesmen !
  Lips of fire and hearts of oak,
How they echoed in the Forum
  Freedom's sounding battle stroke ;
How around our Ark of Safety,
  Like the Israelites of old,
Came they, offering up their treasures,
  Sons and daughters, life and gold.

Oh, my children ! little children !
  These memories come to me,
As after storms the quiet stars,
  Rise o'er the tossing sea ;
Though the grass, and flowers, and streamlets,
  Have lost their tinge of red,
The army still is marching
  To the city of the dead.

And the minute guns are firing
  Like the cadence of a psalm,

And the laurels are transfigured
　To the myrtle and the palm ;
But the rear guard closes upward,
　And the ranks move quickly by
Flags baptized with older glory,
　As they near the beckoning sky.

Betsey Coddington.

About two hundred years ago,
When spring kissed off the winter snow ;
  Under the royal law
Good William Coddington was made,
With all the olden time parade,
  Rhode Island's Governor.

A handsome, courtly man was he,
New England's aristocracy !
  And rich in gold and lands,
With diamond buckles, powdered cue,
Knee breeches, broad-cuffed coat of blue ;
  And ruffles round his hands.

He wore a blood-red signet ring,
With coat of arms and quartering,
  And old heraldic crest ;
A sword with rubied, silver hilt,
And curious gold-embroidered quilt
  Upon his satin vest.

His manners, calm and dignified,
Were tempered with a proper pride

Of goodlie ancestry.
His gabled, quaint old house was known,
With massive chimney built of stone,
  For hospitality.

———

A century gone !—at early dark,
In summer time, the old Town Clerk,
  His dull day's labor done,
Shuts his small office's creaking door;
He bears the honored name o' yore
  Of William Coddington.

Crooked and queer, with eyes that blink,
And hands enstained with truant ink,
  With pleasant, dove-like look ;
Albeit the day is cold or hot—
He travels on a little trot,
  And lugs a ponderous book.

Now by his broad wood fire side,
He chats with a befitting pride,
  Of wills and bonds and deeds;
While Betsey, handsome, tall, and bright,
His child, his household's warmth and light,
  His oft-told wisdom heeds.

She looked and moved a gypsy queen ;
Rare contrast to the quiet scene,
 ᐧAnd low-browed room, was she,
As from a silver tea-pot old,
'Graved with devices manifold
Of " C's " entwined with griffins old,
    She poured the fragrant tea.

———

Years glide like ghosts ; the old Town Clerk
Sleeps 'neath a slate stone, grim and dark,
    And all the folks amazed,
On Sunday after meeting's done,
Gather in groups, and one by one
    Say, " Betsey, she is crazed."

'Twas said a red-cheeked Englishman
Stole her heart's love, and with it ran
    Across the tossing sea.
Be that as't may, nor wind nor gale
Filled with its salt perfume the sail
    That proved his constancy.

So she went mad ; and when the snow
Fell silently, and soft, and slow,
    She stalked the narrow street,

A leafless branch in her brown hand,
Waving it like a witch's wand,
   At those she chanced to meet.

Grotesque and weird her motley guise,
Like coals of fire her glowing eyes ;
   And even boys in fun,
Paused as she passed—always alone—
And whispered in an undertone,
   " Poor Betsey Coddington!"

And so a day in winter came,
When sunset lights its crimson flame,
   On Narragansett's Hill ;
On Coaster's Harbor cold and white,
The poorhouse shines with evening light,
   And Betsey, she is still !

Yes ! stiff, and cold, and stark, and dead,
Upon a pauper's narrow bed ;
And on the white wall at her head,
   Now life's short dream is done,
There hangs a painting, old and rare,
With costume rich, and powdered hair,
   Of Governor Coddington.

And at the poor, worn, weary feet,
That never more will tread the street—
` Safe from all storms and harms,
There is a faded canvass spread,
Strange mockery to the pauper dead,
　Her ancient coat of arms!

The Old Shoemaker.

—

Yes! Jerry he is dead,
And his old-fashioned head
   It lies low;
Where the grass still is green
And the frosts early sheen
   White as snow.

Almost ninety years old,
Straight and queer, strong and bold,
   And how tough;
But his heart it was kind
Like a diamond they find
   In the rough.

How he'd walk the old town,
Where the houses like brown
   Autumn leaves,
Stand all low browed, and quaint
With the sea fog for paint
   On their eaves.

Always talking old times,
Always crooning old rhymes,
  Queer and sage;
Bible maxims he'd quote,
And " Poor Richard " by rote,
  To a page.

When his strength 'gan to wane,
He gave up his stout cane,
  And such things ;
And got ready, he said,
With his good silver head,
  For his wings.

For he always awoke,
When the morning first broke,
  Like a smile ;
Then he perfumed the air,
With a Methodist prayer,
  For a while.

With his thoughts full of love,
For the good God above
  In the sky ;
And of memories sweet,

Of the dear wife he'd meet
  Up on high ;

And his granddaughter, too,
Looking down from the blue
  Like a star,
With a tender surprise
In her beautiful eyes,
  Near and far.

Every week day he'd stalk ;
With his soldierly walk,
  To the shop ;
When his hammer would ring,
And his waxed ends would cling
  While he'd stop

And deliver his views,
On the dreadful abuse
  Of the day.
Of the folly and tricks
Of the folks' politics ;
  Then he'd say,

With a queer sort of frown,
" Now I tell you this town

It has grown,
' Since the day the Stone Mill,
   'Twixt the harbor and hill,
      Stood alone."

Then his mouth he would purse ;
" But its changed for the worse,
   Many ways ;
And its women and men
Aint what they were then ;
   Happy days !
And the folks that I knew,"
Then he'd pound on his shoe,
   " Are all dead."

Then his spectacle bows
He would slowly unclose
   On his head.
When the nine o'clock bell
Rang so clearly and well,
   Overhead,
He would kneel down and pray,
In a patriarch's way,
   By his bed.

And the angels would keep,
Their kind watch in his sleep,
  Through the night ;
While he slumbered and smiled,
And in dreams was a child,
  Till daylight.

But good Jerry is dead,
Autumn leaves brown and red,
  Rustle round.
He left wealth more than gold,
While he sleeps in the old
  Burying ground.

Fragment from Poem

READ BEFORE THE SOCIETY OF THE ARMY OF THE
POTOMAC.

———

It was sunset in October,
   And the sky was all ablaze
With the gorgeous crimson glory
   Of the regal Autumn days ;
Purple banners on the hillside,
   Scarlet pennons on the breeze,
Golden censers rich with incense
   Flaming on the forest trees—
And Potomac's flowing river,
   With its amber tinted tide,
Was jeweled with the splendors
   Of the forest at its side.
But redder glows the sunset
   On the river's gathering tide,
Till forest, stream, and arching sky
   Alike were glorified.
" All was quiet on Potomac !"
   Save the cannon's distant roar,
The neigh of horses in the camp,
   The drum-beat on the shore ;

The tangled notes of trumpets,
  And the clash of falling steel,
The murmuring talk of many men,
  The wagon's rumbling wheel;
The chirping of the meadow birds,
  The crack of teamsters' whips,
The notes of " Rally round the Flag,"
  From soldiers' bearded lips.
" All was quiet on Potomac!"
  In those Indian-summer days,
And battle's sulphury smoke gave place
  To Autumn's purple haze.
The army rested for the night,
  And as the stars came out,
The camp-fire's blazing cheerful light,
  Was gleaming all about.
And foot-worn soldiers gathered round,
  Some stretched at careless ease;
Others broke limbs of resined pine
  From off the nearest trees,
And tossed them on the blazing fire.
  Some sank right down to sleep
With faces placid as a child's,
  When angels guardian keep;
Others roared chorus to a song,

· Some boasted of their deeds;
A fair-haired youth beside the fire,
  His sweetheart's letter reads.
One brawny bummer in a group,
  With voice as clear and strong
As northern gale among the hills,
  Roars out this ringing song;
And all the rest join voices
  When the chorus comes along.

Charles Dickens.

The fog it drifts out, and the fog drifts in,
  But the cable under the sea—
Has thrilled like a wind-moved Æolian harp,
  With its message of sadness to me!
Has echoed and thrilled like a passing bell,
  Which is tolling overhead,
For the magical sceptre has turned to dust—
  The King of Romance is dead.

Oh! red was the flash of the eddying blood,
  That shivered the teeming brain,
And icy the hand that froze the heart
  That never will throb again.
"There is nothing stirring within the room
  But the golden light on the wall;"
And he dreams in his long still sleep perchance,
  Of the children he gave us all.

By the side of the sleeper is "little Nell,"
  And she kisses his silvering hair,
And lovingly touches his cold, cold lips,
  Then melts in the silent air.

And. "Tiny Tim," with angel wings,
   Has dropped his wooden crutch,
And lays his small thin hand upon
   His face with tender touch.

" The child wife" flits across the room,
   In snowy vestments drest,
Her blue eyes filled with pitying tears,
   And nestles in his breast.
" Poor Joe!" all radiant with the light
   That's not on land or sea,
Grasps that kind hand, and then " moves on,"
   To immortality.

And " Little Paul," whose Mother's hand
   Once beckoned him away
Across the river, to the land
   Where there is perfect day ;
Now coming back with gentle grace,
   Soft as the South wind's breath—
Strews fadeless flowers from Heaven's fields,
   On " the old fashion ; Death !"

A lonely "cricket on the hearth,"
   Pipes his shrill requiem there,
The " Chimes " ring out among the stars ;

The blossom-scented air
Seems sweet with the kind memories
Of the dear sleeper there.

Oh! not alone! the pathless path
Leads to our Father's breast ;
Bright angels of the children gone,
Guide him to perfect rest.
And then when merry Christmas comes
On its white wings of snow,
And holly berries glisten red,
And yule log fires glow,
We'll gather in the cheerful light,
And quiet listening there,
Hear the sweet "Christmas Carols" sung
By angels in the air,
And think of him whose boundless love
Draws his dear children there.

Empty Pockets.

Almost two thousand years ago,
   Beside a tranquil sea,
The blessed Saviour walked and talked,
   In ancient Galilee.

No jeweled crown adorned his brow,
   No priestly book or bell,
Within his hand no pilgrim staff,
   No scrip or scallop shell.

Empty his purse of Jewish gold,
   Simple and sad the words,
No place to lay his wearied head,
   Like foxes and the birds.

No leaf-kissed cavern in the woods,
   No nest of silvery moss,—
The manger with its new mown hay;
   Dark Calvary! and the cross.

What tender thoughts arise like stars,
   Within the tranquil mind—

What fragrant memories sweet with love
His teachings leave behind.

No penny with great Cæsar's stamp,
    He tossed the shivering poor;
No scrip he gave the suffering sick
    Who prayed the heavenly cure.

The blind man clutched no Roman coin
    Beneath Judean trees ;
He touched his eyes, who made the light—
    And being blind, he sees.

The sick man very near to death,
    In palsied murmuring talked,
Then gathering life from Jesus' words
    Took up his bed and walked.

The rich man's daughter, white with death,
    Caught healing from the skies—
Flushed with new beauty, at the words,
    " I say to thee, arise !"

The widow following her dead,
    Felt her sad heart rejoice,

When the pale sleeper starts to life
  At the kind Master's voice.

How the poor fallen woman rose,
  When love unknown before,
In tender accents pardoned her ;
  And bade her "Sin no more."

O ! human heart ! thy poverty
  Is no o'ershadowing curse,
For love can crowd with deeds divine
  The slender empty purse.

" Such as I have "—the blessed words
  He spake—" I give to thee ;"
A cup of water in my name
  Is Christian charity."

Rowland Robinson Hazard.

At evening the bright wood fire's light
   Burns up with a cheerful glow,
And there he sits in his great arm-chair,
   With his hair as white as snow,
And the gleam of a smile on his pleasant face
   Which the blessed angels know.

They have lighted the lamps on the old Parade,
   And the State House clock strikes seven,
The great grey trees in the quiet Mall,
   Stand out 'gainst the starry heaven,
And he hums a tune of the better land,
   When the silver chords are riven.

The good wife there in her corner chair,
   Sings snatches of song like a bird—
And the fore-stick breaks with a musical snap,
   And the great red coals are stirred
By the bright brass tongs in his honest hand,
   With a joke and a pleasant word.

His boots are placed on a cricket there
   And his slippers are on his feet—
His newspapers rest on a small round stand,
   And he turns a friend to greet,
With a " Neighbor! how's to do, to-night?"
   In tones that are strangely sweet.

I wish I had a loving hand,
   The dear old scene to paint—
The arches there by the fireside—
   And the great beam strong and quaint,
That bears the low-browed ceiling up,
   Where the shadows flick and faint ;

The andirons, bright as polished gold
   The fenders gleaming brass,
The bronze Napoleon on the shelf,
   The queer Bohemian glass—
And the clock that came from over the seas
   To strike the hours that pass.

The dark, old-fashioned table stands
   By the fond firelight kissed—
Where aged, portly men have played
   Their earnest games of whist—

Silent and serious, till a shout—
   Proclaimed a play that's missed.

Oh! tender days, forever gone—
   White locks beneath white snow,
Oh! dim eyes bright with purer light,
   Our sad hearts only know—
Thy simple, child-like faith has found
   Thy heaven of long ago.

Written in a Worcester Dictionary

PRESENTED TO HIS WIFE'S SISTER ON HER
MARRIAGE.

———

To your husband, this book should have gone,
    For in spite of all rival resisters
He and I when our hope seemed forlorn,
    Have always inclined to *Woo-sisters !*
If a *word* to the wise is enough,
    Why! my gift you will certainly feel—
'Tis a monstrous bouquet of the stuff
    Many *spokes* in a well *tired* wheel.
Words can illy convey the idea
    Though in each there's a *spell* that is *sound,*
Of the blessings with which I now pray,
    Your lives may forever be crowned.
May you *consonant* be to your love,
    May you *vow-ill* in nothing today ;
May you utter no *silly-bulls* here
    When the *hack-sent* shall bear you away.
The red leather binding shall be
    The mythical shoe I will throw,
In a sort of symbolical way,
    My heartfelt good wishes to show.

The Bible you'll find in its leaves,
  And receipt-book and poems and tales,
Most everything bound up in sheaves,
  Talking Jonahs, in taciturn whales.
In your study I hope it may lay,
  In a home-like yet scholarly spot,
When 't will tell you my love all the day
  Whether " Duncan " shall " hear it " or not.

The Old Town Crier.

Well! the New Year came in with a tear and a song
And quaint Johnny Allen came swinging along,
For its nigh fifty years since Town Crier was he
Of pleasant old Newport that smiles by the sea.
And the children stretched out their small mittens
  to touch
His big handled bell and each home-maden crutch,
For his words they were kind, though his voice it
  was rough,
And tender his heart, though his life it was tough.
He had a big head with its white shaggy hair,
And a close fitting cap much too small for his wear.
And his worn coat of homespun had little short
  tails,
That fluttered so drolly in winter's sharp gales.
His body was ponderous and clumsy and strong,
But his legs were put on by mistake and were wrong ;
They were shrivelled and crooked and useless and
  small,
So he might just as well have had no legs at all.
So he stumped through the streets with his crutches
  and bell,

And he cried for a living, but laughed just as well.

Olden ballads he sold for a copper apiece,

On the Newport Bank steps, with a heart full of
     peace ;

And he daily thanked God, and asked no one for
     aid,

But drank from the fountain down on the Parade.

Then he'd croak out the notes like a big Katy-did,

Of sweet " Betsey Baker " and bold " Captain Kidd."

I heard him one night when the storm rattled wild,

He was crying the loss of a poor little child ;

And I turned in my bed and my heart gave a throb

For his bell seemed to moan and his voice seemed
     to sob.

I never have known just the time when he died,

For the void that he left was not aching or wide.

But I hope with the angels new ballads he sings,

And his crutches have blossomed and turned into
     wings.

Two Graves by the Sea.

I wonder if the people think,
Driving along the Ocean's brink,
  When sunset's rose is red,
Of where the water almost laves
The silent, solitary graves
  Of the forgotten dead?

Two graves alone—all, all alone!
Marked with a rudely graven stone,
  Beside the moaning waves;
The simple stories briefly tell,—
Instead of flowers, a white sea shell
  Rests on the sunken graves.

Almost an hundred years are gone,
With starry eve and crimson morn,
  Since the wild stormy day
When broken spars and shattered deck,
All gashed and gored—a helpless wreck,
  The ship was cast away.

The fishers in their little skiff,
Beneath the brown sea-weeded cliff,
  Drift with the swelling tide;

And as the sunset glories fade,
A glittering bright-hued cavalcade,
  Pause by the cool seaside.

The spray has shed its briny tears,
Where yonder rock its gray head rears,
  And in the dell beyond
White lilies with their crowns of gold,
Float fresh with perfumes manifold
  Upon the glassy pond.

Along the roadside's fern-decked brush,
The sweet wild roses bloom and blush,
  Lilies arrayed like kings,
With royal purple hues intense,
Nod—while the blackbirds on the fence
  Flutter with flame-tipped wings.

The light-ship on the horizon's rim,
As evening shadows gather dim,
  Rolls, beckoning to the night ;
Unclosed its quivering eyes of flame
From the great lantern's iron frame,
  Like stars of ruddy light.

I wonder *when* the farmers found
The ship-wrecked sailors stiff and drowned,

Upon the pebbled shore,
And drew them from the gurgling tide,
To place them kindly, side by side,
  Beyond the great waves' roar.

Mayhap they perished in the night,
When skies were black and ocean white,
  With gleaming tawny foam ;
And how convulsively they clutched
The slippery, weedy rocks they touched,
  And thought of friends and home.

Mayhap for years their loved ones watched,
From vine-clad cots, all white and thatched,
  Upon a sunny shore,
For the dear sailors on the main,
Who never will come back again,
  No ! not forevermore.

In the old town, the distant bells
Ring faintly sweet,-- the ocean swells
  And breaks with saddening moan ;
The quiet stars shine on the sand,
And there beside the sea they stand ;
  Two graves, and one gray stone.

Fragment from a Poem

READ BEFORE ST. JOHN'S LODGE.

———

It was autumn in the Rhine-land,
   And along the river side,
The purple grapes were hanging
   O'er the rippling, glassy tide,
Till the very wind seemed drunken,
   And went singing on its way,
Among the bending, vineyard trees,
   A jovial roundelay :
And the Heidelberg's old towers
   All in the distance stood,
Like giants in the sunset,
   With their hair all moist with blood ;
And the windows seemed of silver,
   And the spires made of gold,
While the vesper-bells were ringing,
   A ballad-tune of old.
Then up the moon came marching,
   With a banner made of light,
And quiver filled with silver spears,
   To guard the halls of night :

Then the shadows in the city
  Grew phantom-like and dim,
Whilst down the great cathedral's aisle
  Faint grew the evening hymn,
Where the painted Gothic windows
  Drank up the sunset light,
And thus it was in Heidelberg
  Came down the *holy night.*
In yonder moss-grown castle,
  That standeth all alone,
Like a knight of ancient heraldry,
  Gigantic, turned to stone,—
To guard the swelling bosom
  Of the sunset blushing Rhine,
There sat four German students,
  And they drank the ruby wine;
Adown their beards it trickled
  In gems of glittering pride—
For they drank a flowing bumper
  To their loves and to the bride
They each had sworn to honor,
  Till the sands of life were gone;
The angel of the temple-gate;
  The memory of *St. John.*
And then up spake the eldest,

And a student great was he,
For his mind was stored with learning
As with jewels is the sea.
He could tell a goodly story,
    And he had as great a heart;
As Heidelberg and Swabia's
    Fair cities are apart.
" My brothers!" quoth the student,
    " The day is almost gone,
That we have kept with festive rites,
    To honor good *St. John ;*
The sun in all its glorious path,
    Knows scarce a land on earth—
That does not celebrate the time
    That gave our patron birth ;
But I have read a strange legend—
    All in a little book,
With silver clasps and vellum leaves,
    And *yellow, time-worn look;*
The author's name has passed away,
    The book remaineth here,
Brought by an ancient pilgrim's hand
    Away from far Judea ;
Once on a time, I heard, 'twas found,
    When the great war begun,

By a rude soldier, in a tomb,
   Beside a skeleton ;
The bony hand still clutched it tight,
   And rattled as it fell
To the damp ground ; if living now
   What stories it might tell."

    *   *   *   *   *   *

But dark and darker grew the night
   Within the Gothic room,
And closer yet the students pressed
   Amid the gathering gloom ;
The speaker's voice rang strangely out
   Upon the silent air,
And the grim shadows rose and fell,
   And beckoned everywhere.
" My Brothers!" thus the legend ran,
   Preserved by Jewish seers,
" The good *St. John* comes *back to earth*
   Once in a hundred years.
The burden of a cross he bears ;
   His hair is very white—
Then let us watch till the high twelve,
   For he *may* come to-night."

    *   *   *   *   *   *

" 'T is well! 't is well!" thus spake they all,
   In voices very low ;
And on the air the tide of night
   So heavily did flow,
That phantoms seemed to fill the room,
And float within the gathering gloom,
   And glide them to and fro.

*   *   *   *   *   *

Past ten o'clock! The moon went down
   In a great flood of light,
And drew its silver mantle
   From the dark-eyed sleeping night.
Eleven ! and the iron tongue
   In the cathedral tower,
Was chiming out, with groan and shout,
   The death of the passing hour ;
The scud was flitting across the sky,
Like the mists that pass o'er the closing eye
Of the strong man lying down to die ;—
   An hour is gone
   To the mystical bourne,
 " From whence no traveler returns,"
   And up in the arch of the evening air,
   The old clock's hands are clasped in prayer,

As they slowly rise to the angel skies,
  And *twelve* of the midnight is everywhere.
Hark! to the rushing of viewless wings,
Beating the air in their wanderings;
Listen, the chime of the convent bells,
Catching the story the old clock tells—
One in the great cathedral's tower,
Chanting and tolling the midnight hour—
And the other away on the banks of the Rhine,
Where under the stars the ripples shine,
And the evergreens shadow the Virgin's shrine.

Job B. Wilbour.

As one by one, old Newport's worthies die,
And of their death, I read the notice brief,
Our pleasant city seems an ancient tree
Shedding it's autumn foliage leaf by leaf.
  Though tender verdure soon may deck the plain,
  These russet leaves will never green again.

Job Wilbour dead! life's time-piece all run down.
What pleasant memories of his little shop,
Where sunshine lingered on the work bench brown,
And watches ticked as if they'd never stop.
  While moon and stars rose on the clock's great
    face
  Decked with gray cobwebs on its dusty case.

I see him now, short, stout, with shaggy head,
A silvery laugh that made the watches ring,
Hung on a wire across the window pane.
A story good he'd tell; a few strains sing
  Of an old tune he carrolled when a boy,
  For Job's great heart was full of light and joy.

Now, with his glass screwed in his twinkling eye,
He'd swift dissect a tarnished bull's eyes heart,
Then in bewildering maze, ingeniously
With cunning hand pluck all the wheels apart.
    The sunbeams nestling on his half bowed head.
    They kiss his grave to-day, for Job is dead!

How oft th' old-fashioned door with a rattling jar,
Opened a moment wide its upper half,
And from the steps a cheery friend looked in,
To tell a story and to have a laugh!
    To set his watch, for Job would say in fun,
    By my old clock they regulate the sun.

His time is out, his busy hands are still ;
No artisan can mend the worn out spring,
The weight-cord broken when the clock struck
        twelve!
The face is shadowed by an angel's wing.
    Eternity! unmeasured is thy day,
    Then be ye also ready, " Watch and pray!"

The Boat Builder's Shop.

The Summer sunset blossoms like a rose,
Blushing and fragrant ; at the day's sweet close
   I loiter in my evening walk, and stop—
On the Long Wharf, that stretches far away,
Into the waters of the sleeping bay
   At the wide doors of the Boat Builder's shop.

On the horizon's reddening, breathing lips
Like smiles come sailing up the little ships,
   Sea birds, and land birds circle in the air,
I hear the dip of oars, the laugh of girls,
The shouts the bearded sailor gives as close he furls
   His half-reluctant sails to winds not fair.

The grey town half asleep dreamily tells
Its lullaby in the clear evening bells,
   A snowy fragrant lily closed at dark,
Trinity's tall spire—slim and white
Lifts toward celestial lands its crown of light
   Gemmed with the dying sunset's vital spark.

When the sweet evening breath blows cool and damp
Alladin in the light house rubs his lamp,
    Kindling its flame above the rolling sea,
And in the glow beyond the purple land,
The waves transmuted by its silver wand
    Gleam with bright jewels sparkling radiantly.

The restless tide laps on the slippery piles,
Moss grown and swaying; and in broken files
    The wild geese clank their slender blackening
      chain
Up towards the zenith ; and like winged snow·—
The coral footed gulls sweep high and low,
    Their downy breasts wet from the foaming main.

In the Boat Builder's shop the master stands
With weather beaten face, and sun burned hands,
    Half sailor, and half landsman quaint is he ;
The tender light of home within his eye,
But every breath he breathes, and every sigh
    Is perfumed with the odors of the sea.

A stout sea captain with a rolling walk
Leans on an anchor for a pleasant talk,
Watching the tarry handed men who calk

An upturned boat upon the pebbled shore.
Squat on the fragment of a broken mast,
A sailor croons his stories of the past,
 Gilded with romance brighter than before.

Now from the Fort booms down the Sunset gun,
Lights gleam within the windows, one by one ;
 With creaking rolling sound, the heavy door
Shuts in the skeletons of boats to be—
And the grey fog crawls from the silver sea—
Like the dead sailor's ghosts mysteriously—
 And sheds its salt sea tears upon the shore.